<u>An Introduction to French Furniture of the 17th and 18th-Century</u>

Including Chapters on Louis Quatorze, Louis Quinze and the Regency

By

Frederick Litchfield

D1241986

British Library Cataloguing-in-Publication Data
A catalogue record for this book is available from
the British Library

A History of Furniture

Furniture is the mass noun for the movable objects intended to support various human activities, such as seating, storing, working and sleeping. Most often, at least in the present day - furniture is the product of a lengthy design process and considered a form of decorative art. In addition to furniture's functional role, it can also serve a symbolic or religious purpose, for instance in churches, temples or shrines. It can be made from many materials, including metal, plastic, and wood - using a variety of techniques, joins and decoration, reflecting the local culture from which it originated.

Furniture has been a part of the human experience since the development of non-nomadic cultures, and even before this in its crudest form. Evidence of furniture survives from the Neolithic Period and later in antiquity in the form of paintings, such as the wall Murals discovered at Pompeii; sculpture, and examples have been excavated in Egypt and found in tombs in Ghiordes, in modern-day Turkey. Perhaps one of the most interesting archaeological sites is Skara Brae, a Neolithic village located in Orkney (an archipelago in northern Scotland). The site dates from 3100–2500 BC and due to a shortage of wood in Orkney, the people of Skara Brae were forced to build with stone, a readily available material that could be worked easily and turned into household items. Each house shows a high degree of sophistication and was equipped with an extensive assortment of stone furniture, ranging from cupboards, dressers and beds to shelves, stone seats, and limpet tanks. The stone dresser was regarded as the most important item, as it symbolically faced the entrance in each house and was therefore the first item seen when entering.

The furniture of the Middle Ages was usually heavy, oak, and ornamented with carved designs. Along with the other arts, the Italian Renaissance of the fourteenth and fifteenth century marked a rebirth in design, often inspired by the Greco-Roman tradition. A similar explosion of design, and renaissance of culture in general, occurred in Northern Europe, starting in the fifteenth century. The seventeenth century, in both Southern and Northern Europe, was characterized by opulent, often gilded Baroque designs that frequently incorporated a profusion of vegetal and scrolling ornament. Starting in the eighteenth century, furniture designs began to develop more rapidly. Although there were some styles that belonged primarily to one nation, such as 'Palladianism' in Great Britain (derived from and inspired by the designs of the Venetian architect Andrea Palladio) or 'Louis Quinze' in French furniture (characterised by supreme craftsmanship and the integration of the arts of cabinet-making, painting, and sculpture), others, such as 'Rococo' and 'Neoclassicism' were perpetuated throughout Western Europe.

The nineteenth century is usually defined by concurrent revival styles, including Gothic, Neoclassicism, and Roccoco. The design reforms of the late century introduced the 'Aesthetic movement' (essentially promoting the beauty of objects above any other social or political themes) and the 'Arts and Crafts movement' (An international design movement that flourished between 1860-1910, led by William Morris. It stood for traditional craftsmanship using simple form, often applying medieval, romantic or folk styles of decoration). Art Nouveau, in turn was influenced by both of these movements. This latter development was perhaps the most influential of all, inspired by natural forms and structures; evident primarily in architecture, but also the beautiful objects crafted to fill such spaces. Noted furniture designers in this style included William H. Bradley; the 'Dean of American Designers', Goerges de Feure, the Parisian designer who famously produced the theatre designs for *Le Chat Noir* cabaret, and Hermann Obrist, a German sculptor of the Jugendstil (the German branch of Art Nouveaux) movement.

The first three-quarters of the twentieth century are often seen as the march towards Modernism in furniture design. Modernism, in general, includes the activities and creations of those who felt traditional forms of art, architecture, literature, religious faith and social activities were becoming outdated in the new economic, social, and political environment of an emergent industrialized world. Art Deco, De Stijl, Bauhaus, Wiener Werkstätte, and Vienna Secession designers all worked to some degree within the Modernist idiom. Born from the Bauhaus and Art Deco/Streamline styles came the post WWII 'Mid-Century Modern' style using materials developed during the war including laminated plywood, plastics and fibreglass. Prime examples include furniture designed by George Nelson Associates, Charles and Ray Eames, Paul McCobb and Danish modern designers including Finn Juhl and Arne Jacobsen. Post-modern design, intersecting the Pop art movement, gained steam in the 1960s and 70s, promoted in the 1980s by groups such as the Italy-based Memphis movement. The latter group worked with ephemeral designs, featuring colourful decoration and asymmetrical shapes.

As is evident from this short history, the history of artistic developments is inextricably linked with the progression of furniture design. This is hardly surprising, as after all, many artists, thinkers and designers would stringently resist any artificial separation between traditional fine art and functional design. Both respond to their wider context and environment, both, perhaps in differing ways, seeking to impact on reality and society.

Today, British professional furniture makers have self organised into a strong and vibrant community, largely under the organisation 'The Worshipful Company of Furniture Makers', commonly referred to as the Furniture Makers or the Furniture Makers Company. Its motto is 'Straight and Strong'! Members of the Company come from many professions and disciplines, but the common link is that all members on joining must be engaged in or with the UK furnishing industry. Thus the work of the Company is delivered by members with wide ranging professional knowledge and skills in manufacturing, retailing, education, journalism; in fact any aspect of the industry. There are many similar organisations across the globe, as well as in the UK, all seeking to integrate and promote the valuable art that is furniture making. Education is a key factor in such endeavours, and maintaining strong links between professional practitioners, didactic colleges and the amateur maker/restorer is crucial. We hope the reader enjoys this book.

Contents

	Page No.
Introduction	1
Louis Quatorze	4
The Regency Period	12
Louis Quinze	13
The Directory	27
Reproductions	33

FRENCH FURNITURE

Change from Gothic to Renaissance—Furniture of Louis XIII period. LOUIS QUATORZE—Public collections of French furniture of this period—Berain and Lebrun—André Charles Boulle, his work and methods—Boulle's successors—Reproductions by eminent makers, *première et contre partie*—Marqueterie of West Indian veneers, designs of Riesener—Chinese lacquer used for furniture. THE REGENCY PERIOD—Change in style and characteristic ornaments of the time. LOUIS QUINZE— Change in French manners and customs—Caffieri and his work —The subjects of tapestry used for furniture—Introduction of lighter articles, and descriptions of them. LOUIS SEIZE AND MARIE ANTOINETTE—Influence of the Queen—Change of fashion—Pierre Gouthière and his work—Vernis Martin—Style of panels and difference in treatment of interior decorations. THE DIRECTORY—Changes brought about by the Revolution— Pseudo-classicalism of the period—The National Convention. THE FIRST EMPIRE—Napoleon as Caesar—Introduction of Egyptian ornament—Characteristic features of furniture of the time—Massive carved and gilt chairs—Furniture subsequent to the time of Napoleon. REPRODUCTIONS—Different kinds of reproductions of the best pieces—Remarks and suggestions.

IN France, as in other countries, the mediaeval period of art gave way to fifteenth-century Gothic. In such beautiful monuments of delicate tracery in stone-work as Rouen Cathedral, we can see to what perfection of design and intricate detail, the French architect and craftsman could manipulate the stone of Caen. The woodwork interiors, and such furniture of a movable kind as

1

w:re in use in those early days, followed the lines of the stone-work, and French Gothic wood-carving was unsurpassed. Unfortunately very few examples remain after the lapse of nearly five hundred years, and it is only by studying such fragments of panels, mouldings and carved ornament, as are to be found in the collection of Emile Peyre, very wisely purchased by the Victoria and Albert Museum a few years ago, that we can estimate the merit of wood-carving in France of the fifteenth century.

In the chapter on Renaissance furniture, some reference has been made to the great change that came about in Italy during the fifteenth century, and was carried to France during the reign of François Premier. During the lifetime of this king and his successors, the Renaissance movement in art, and particularly in stone and woodwork, held sway with varying taste, from pure to debased, but for the purpose of this handbook we can only give a rapid glance at this century of art progress, and hurry on to a time nearer our own, of which there are more examples preserved to us.

For those who would study the furniture of the French Renaissance, there are excellent works by able authors, and the Cluny Museum contains beautiful specimens of the best and also of the later periods. Besides those which are in such public collections, there are few pieces of really authentic furniture of this time to be found. Occasionally what appears to be an old buffet, chair, or credence comes to light, but a careful examination will generally reveal the fact, that, while a panel or a piece of carved ornament is of the period, the remainder has been made in the style of such a piece of furniture as was evidently suggested by the genuine old fragments.

During the reign of Louis Treize, furniture became more comfortable, and there was more variety. The chairs were high-backed, and were, for the

ARMCHAIR IN TAPESTRY (EARLY LOUIS QUATORZE)

first time, made with arms; the legs and stretchers were visible and were of oak or walnut wood, the high backs and seats were covered with tapestry from the looms of Beauvais. There is a kind of marqueterie which we now identify with this period; it is rich in tone and full of design—the scheme of decoration being a number of panels or cartouches with baskets or bouquets of flowers in each panel; the mountings, if there be any, are of carved and gilt wood, instead of the cast and chased gilt bronze which came into fashion some fifty years later. In the Victoria and Albert Museum there is a cabinet of this style and period deserving careful attention.

Louis Quatorze

After Louis XIV came to the throne a new era may be said to have begun for French decorative art, and in the palaces of Versailles, the Louvre, the *Musée du Garde Meuble*, and in such collections as that lately given to the nation by Lady Wallace, and the Jones Bequest in South Kensington, we have proofs of the degree to which the manufacture of sumptuous and elegant furniture was carried. Under the superintendence of Colbert, the king's minister of finance, the most generous encouragement was given to artists and skilled craftsmen, and the making of gorgeous furniture was raised to the level of painting and sculpture. Orders were given for special designs, and cabinet makers were encouraged by royal patronage and favour, being honoured by such newly-coined titles as *Maître Ebeniste* and *Ebeniste au Roi*. Immense sums of money were expended to produce those magnificent examples of the cabinet maker's art and industry, justly entitled to the description *Meubles de luxe*.

Berain and Lebrun furnished the designs executed by André Charles Boulle, his sons and successors, and the kind of furniture identified with his name, but which has since become vulgarized and

4

common, came into fashion. The process adopted by Boulle is pretty well known, but can scarcely be passed by without a word of explanation. The design was enlarged from the original drawing into

ARMCHAIR IN TAPESTRY (LOUIS QUATORZE)
A little later than the preceding illustration

a full-sized diagram, and then cut out in sheets of tortoise-shell and brass, prepared beforehand for the purpose. Such portions of the design as were intended to remain in brass were then eliminated from the sheet of tortoise-shell, and a similar plan was adopted with the brass which it was intended to replace with tortoise-shell. The two sheets of different materials thus treated were then pressed into each other, much in the same way that we have seen children's puzzle pictures and maps, when the design of the paper picture of which the puzzle is a copy has been completed. A strong solution of glue was well brushed into the crevices between brass and shell; paper was then laid over the work, and it was allowed to get hard and dry. In a day or two the paper would be scraped off, and the Boulle work, which I should have mentioned had already been laid upon the foundation of the piece of furniture it was proposed to ornament, would be ready for scraping, rubbing down and polishing. The engraving of the surface thus prepared was a very important branch of the work; the design was, to use a technical term, "blind," until the deft hand of the artist-engraver gave it life. For an instance let us take the well-known design in old Boulle work which we call the "squirrel" pattern, because part of its ornament consists of that little animal represented in brass inlay. That portion of thin brass which is part of the sheet I have described, would simply represent the shape of the squirrel until a little shading, the indication of paws, tail, eye and other touches from the engraver's tool, here and there, had given the squirrel form and life. It is the same with each figure, each scroll and flower, so that it must be obvious that much of the merit and spirit of the work, depends upon the skill of the engraver. When this process was complete a black pigment like thick ink was rubbed into the lines made by the graver, which showed up all the details of the design, and this, having the dark shell

FRENCH KNEEHOLE TABLE BY ANDRÉ CHARLES BOULLE
(LOUIS QUATORZE)

as a background, made a rich picture. Boulle may be black, red or brown; sometimes pieces are enriched by panels of blue, and I have seen panels of green. These colours are produced by placing underneath the veneer, a colouring matter which shows through the transparent portions of the tortoise-shell, a material which everyone knows is partly opaque and partly transparent. Under the shell, which was intended to remain brown, gilding was sometimes introduced to heighten the effect. In the panels of a piece of furniture which the *ébeniste* intended to be more fanciful, he would sometimes insert a piece of horn, which, unlike the shaded effect of tortoiseshell, was wholly transparent; under this horn he would place a grayish blue colour, which would come as a relief to the black boulle and produce a very decorative effect.

The furniture made by Boulle in this manner was further ornamented by massive mountings of gilt bronze; some of the beautiful cabinets in the Louvre have figures in high relief, scrolls, birds, and ornamental mouldings standing out from the surface of the boulle work. The handles of the chests of drawers or commodes are massive and handsome. The reader will find the best productions of boulle in the Louvre "Galerie d'Apollon," in the Jones Bequest at South Kensington, and in the Wallace Collection at Hertford House, Manchester Square, London.

Long after Boulle and his sons and successors had passed away, and years after his work had gone out of fashion, a revival of the taste for this highly decorative furniture came about, and boulle-work, or buhl, as it is more generally written and pronounced, was made by several firms in London and Paris. Of course, save for the fact that the process invented by the originator has been adopted, there is not much real similarity between a showy buhl table made in London or Paris, and sold for from fifteen to thirty pounds, and the magnificent boulle armoire in the Jones Bequest, which cost that collector about £5,000.

Quite apart from this modern and cheaper class of buhl there are reproductions of the fine old pieces made in Paris by such first-class makers as Zwiener, Beurdelet, Dasson, and one or two others; these are really on the lines of the old work, well made and of fine finish, and worth purchasing by those who admire the style, but are unable or unwilling to pay enormous prices for what are practically museum specimens.

More will be said presently about these first-class reproductions of museum specimens, but before dismissing Boulle work I will explain a little matter which often puzzles amateurs.

When the sheets of shell and brass are cut and, as already explained, certain portions of each material are withdrawn, so that the designs may be completed in the respective proportions of each material which were arranged in the original drawing, these deleted pieces of brass and shell remain over as a surplus. In some instances these were discarded altogether, and sold to smaller makers; in the majority of cases they were used for the side panels of a cabinet, where they would not be so much *en évidence*, or they were made up into a piece of furniture corresponding in form to the original piece, but the relative portions of the design would be exactly the reverse of the original—where was brass would now be shell, and *vice versâ*.

This kind of buhl was called *contre partie*, sometimes by English cabinet makers I have heard the two parts called "positive" and "negative," or distinguished as "male" and "female"; and I remember a very amusing incident in which a lady asked me for the explanation of the puzzling remark which a certain connoisseur colonel, a friend of hers, had made, by telling her that her buhl card table was only the "feminine" kind. Of course this kind of buhl, which the French more appropriately term the *contre partie*, is of much less value than the *première partie*, or first selection of the cut sheets of the design.

The importation of different choice woods from the West Indies no doubt encouraged the production of marqueterie furniture. A rich dark West Indian wood, something like Rosewood, darker than mahogany, was called *bois du roi*, or "Kingwood," because it was favoured by the king. A yellowish and striped veneer was called "tulip" wood because its pretty variegated appearance somewhat resembled the colours of the common tulip. Holly-tree wood stained different colours, Citron, Coromandel, Brazil, Zebra wood, Sandal, and other fancy and variegated veneers, were used to give colour and variety to the marqueterie enrichment of the furniture of the time.

The designs were numerous and diverse; sometimes the veneers of the same wood were placed different ways of the grain or figure, so that the four sections of a panel would have the figure pointing towards the centre, the outer edge of the panel being banded by a different, generally a darker wood, with a key pattern or other design as a framework. The panel would sometimes contain a trophy of musical instruments, a basket of flowers, or a landscape. Riesener, one of the first *ébenistes* of the time of Louis XV and his successor, affected a box-pattern marqueterie as a groundwork of some of his pieces. He also made some of his beautiful cabinets in three compartments, the centre one slightly projecting and having a panel inlaid with a vase of flowers, while the side compartments slightly receded and were ornamented by the lozenge-shaped squares or diamonds which were a favourite form of decoration with him.

Lacquered panels and boxes had been brought from China and Japan by collectors and merchants; these were taken to pieces and parts mounted into the furniture of the period, but as there was considerable difficulty in procuring the lacquer from Tonking or Fouchow, the clever French craftsman was not long before he contrived to produce a similar article, and this he used in the panels of his tables, secretaires, and commodes. Mounting in gilt bronze completed the ornamental enrichment of the furniture of the Louis Quatorze period. These mounts are of dignified and restrained designs; the broken scroll is a characteristic ornament, the curves are graceful, and generally the work is stately and massive; slabs of rare marbles and of Egyptian porphyry surmounted some of the sumptuous pieces.

The Regency Period

After the death of the *Grand Monarque*, as Louis XIV was called, a style for decoration and furniture came into vogue termed *l'époque de la Régence*. It marks a change which took place during the infancy of the grandson of the late king, the curves and scrolls are more free, and a characteristic form of ornamentation is the frequent introduction of the heads and busts of women with the head-dress of the period, made in gilt bronze, and enriching the marqueterie commodes, tables and cabinets of the time.

Louis Quinze

About this period, and during the reign of Louis XV the manners and customs of the French aristocracy underwent a change; it was the age of the Boudoir rather than of the *Salon de Réception*, with smaller rooms, in which people lived and talked, and naturally there was smaller and less cumbrous furniture. The family of Martin made their famous *Vernis Martin* panels, enriching the more fanciful furniture of the period, metal mountings became more ornate and highly chased and finished, and towards the latter part of the reign decoration and wood-work became rococo and over-ornate, and design, which in the time of Louis Quatorze had been dignified, became debased by redundant and excessive ornament, a salient feature being the conventionalized curled endive.

Caffieri was the most famous mounter in bronze of this period, and was largely employed by King and Court. His designs were quaint, but somewhat rococo, introducing the Chinese mandarin and dragon, the pagoda and other eccentricities into his scheme of ornamentation. Monkeys playing with a skipping rope, and other odd and curious conceptions, gave to his designs a fanciful and grotesque effect, but possessing great merit by reason of the vigour and spirit of the work. Any piece of furniture mounted by Caffieri now realizes an enormous price, but copies of his designs, with the exception of those made by first-class makers, lack all the merits of his original work, and are only frivolous and rococo pieces of metal enrichment, appealing to those who like plenty of ornament, but are not too critical as to its quality.

As the habits of French society became more social and less formal, the fashion of furniture followed suit. Instead of the stately *fauteuil* of Louis Quatorze, we have the word *chaise* as a diminutive of *chaire* coming into vogue, and in place of the tapestry covering of Beauvais, with representations of a boar hunt or the chase, we have the looms of Aubusson or of Gobelins, furnishing the smaller and more domestic subjects for tapestry coverings. La Fontaine's fables, bouquets of flowers, representations of courtly gentlemen and charming ladies conversing or dancing, are the subjects for the *chaises,* the *fauteuils,* the *canapés,* and *bergères* of the period. The *canapé* was a sofa or settee large enough to hold three persons, as distinct from the *causeuse,* which only accommodated two. The *bonheur du jour,* a little cabinet table suitable for a lady's room, came in about this time. The *cartonnière,* a table with an arrangement for the storage of papers; the *escritoire* of a lighter description than formerly, the *chaise-longue,* and other useful and decorative articles were made during this reign. Our own comfortable English sofa, the " Chesterfield," has no counterpart in French furniture; and the *chaise-longue* is the nearest approach to a lounge.

The *canapé,* or French sofa, is by no means a

FRENCH COMMODE, PROBABLY BY CRESSENT, WITH FINE GILT MOUNTS
(LOUIS QUINZE)

15

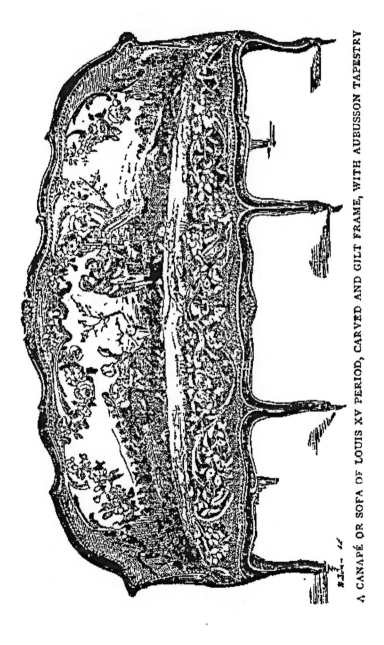

A CANAPÉ OR SOFA OF LOUIS XV PERIOD, CARVED AND GILT FRAME, WITH AUBUSSON TAPESTRY

17

luxurious seat, being to all intents and purposes an upholstered settee, which, however beautiful and valuable its tapestry covering, would not rest the tired owner, like our own English sofa.

FAUTEUIL OF LOUIS XV PERIOD, CARVED AND GILT FRAME
COVERED WITH AUBUSSON TAPESTRY

A French suite of furniture of this period comprised the *canapé*, two or four *fauteuils* or armchairs, and four or six single chairs, or *chaises*. The accessory furniture would be the above-mentioned *chaise-longue*, a pair of *bergères*, which were easy chairs with padded arms, and perhaps some elegant footstools with carved and gilt frames.

FRENCH OCCASIONAL TABLES WITH GILT MOUNTS
LOUIS SEIZE

Louis Seize and Marie Antoinette

It is not until the beautiful bride of the Dauphin, Marie Antoinette, had made her influence a power

FAUTEUIL OF LOUIS XVI PERIOD, CARVED AND GILT FRAME
WITH AUBUSSON TAPESTRY

over fashion, that the taste for the frivolity and excess of ornamentation was checked. A severer tone was made to prevail in matters of taste, in dress, in decoration and in furniture. The *cabriole* or scroll-formed leg was gradually abandoned in favour of the straight and tapering support of chair, table and cabinet. Plain mahogany with simple flutings ornamented with husks, or white painted furniture relieved by gilding, came into vogue. Sometimes the simplicity of design and material was compensated by lavish expenditure of time and skill in the details of the beautiful gilt bronze mountings which have made the *Meubles de luxe* of this time so remarkable.

Pierre Gouthière was the most famous mounter of this reign, as was Caffieri of the preceding one, and he has left us some of the most beautiful pieces of furniture that the world possesses. Three of the most remarkable examples of this master were sold in 1882 at the famous Hamilton Palace sale for about £30,000.

The Vernis Martin panels of the time of Marie Antoinette, were decorated by and after Pater, instead of the cupids and nymphs by Boucher which had pleased the fancy of Mesdames du Barri and Pompadour. The small round table, the *guéridon*, the little work table, and more dainty and better designed furniture became the rage. Sèvres china plaques were used to enrich the secretaires and cabinets of the best makers. The panelling of rooms, the chimney-pieces, cornices and mouldings were simple, a riband and a rose entwined, or a trophy formed of Hymen's torches bound by a garland of roses; pilasters, flat and fluted, with husks as ornaments in the flutings; panels, either square or having what is termed by architects a " broken corner," with a round patera where the corner of the panel is so broken; these are all features of the *boiseries*, or panelled interiors, which

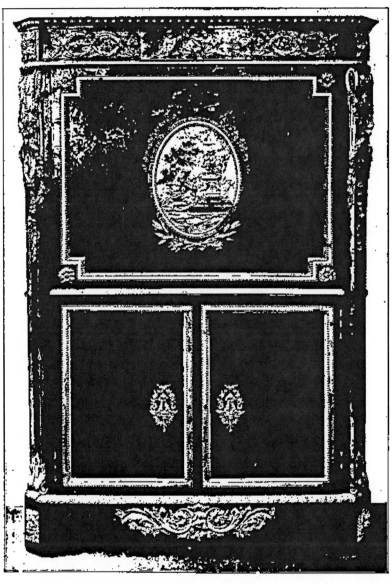

FRENCH UPRIGHT ESCRITOIRE, MOUNTED BY GOUTHIÈRE
TIME OF LOUIS SEIZE

23

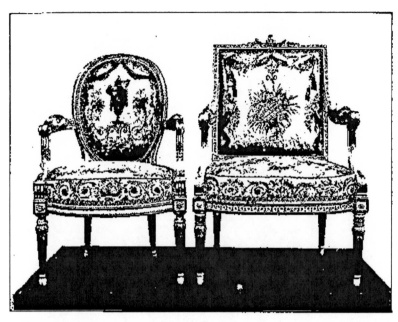

FRENCH FAUTEUILS, CARVED AND GILT FRAMES WITH AUBUSSON TAPESTRY
LOUIS SEIZE

FRENCH MARQUETERIE COMMODE BY RIESENER
LOUIS SEIZE

were the fashion of the day, replacing the lavish use of the rococo scroll, and the curled endive ornament of the latter part of the Louis XV period.

The Directory

A great deal might be written about the beautiful furniture of Marie Antoinette's time, and in my " Illustrated History of Furniture " I have devoted more space to this important period of French industrial art; but for the purposes of this slight review we must press on.

The great Revolution brought about a change in the style of furniture as in everything else. Between the period of those terrible tragedies which marked this great historical catastrophe and that of the First Empire, there was a period known as the *Directoire*. The style of this time was marked by a mixture of the lines of the period which had just passed away, and an affectation of the classicalism of ancient Rome. We find *torchères* of tripod form with a serpent coiling round the centre support; clocks and candelabra the supports of which are seated griffins; the same mystic emblem of an old world mythology serves as the support of a table, and Caryatides figures stiff in posture, form the pilasters of cabinets. These are some of the characteristic ornaments of this period of taste.

The plainer or more domestic furniture of simple mahogany, or of white painted wood, was not materially altered from the Louis Seize designs; the metal mounts, if any, would be a little more stiff and formal, but they would scarcely be distinguishable from those of the previous style, unless marked by some detail which showed this classic influence. The reader will remember that the years were renumbered and the months renamed by the National Convention, which was to destroy monarchies and set up republics in their place. Naturally we find some evidence of this pseudo-classicalism in the decoration and furniture of the short life of Directory government.

A FIRST EMPIRE CHAIR

The First Empire

Then followed the Napoleonic period. As first Consul and afterwards as Emperor, Napoleon I loved to pose as Caesar; his portraits by Canova in marble represent him as a Roman Emperor crowned with a garland of bay leaves; and in war and politics the rôle of a Roman conqueror seems to have possessed him. The imperial stamp is on

FRENCH CHAIR AND SOFA OF THE FIRST EMPIRE PERIOD

everything, and we find the idea of copying the models and shapes of antique Greece and Rome developed and more pronounced than during his consulate. In 1798 Buonaparte, as the general of the Directory, had fought the battle of the Pyramids, and this gives us a date for the introduction of the sphinx and other Egyptian ornaments into French decorative art; later on we find this Egyptian influence, together with the Greek and Roman ornament, paramount. Stiff-winged figures holding garlands of victory, their feet close together like those of the Egyptian bronzes; animals' feet adapted to ornament the legs of chairs and tables; the conventionalized honeysuckle ornament, which originated in Egypt and was adopted by Greece, used as a frieze for table or cabinet; these are all favourite decorative emblems of this time. The furniture itself was generally made of simple but richly-figured Spanish mahogany, stiff in form and classic in type; mahogany columns formed the legs of tables, and had capitals and bases of gilt bronze. Stiffly-draped figures of Terpsichore or her sister Muses, winged female figures, garlands, chariots of Roman conquerors or eagles, Roman fasces, griffins or sphinxes were salient ornaments. Lions' heads formed the handles and their feet adorned the bases of furniture. Whatever difficulty there may be in deciding between some of the earlier styles, there need not be much hesitation in assigning French furniture of this type to that of the late time of the Directory or to that of the First Empire. There is one great merit that this rather aggressive kind of furniture possesses, and that is the excellent quality of the work itself: cabinet work, chasing, gilding, all are good of their kind. The more

ordinary and domestic furniture followed the lines
of the richer descriptions. Instead of the mounts

A MASSIVE CARVED AND GILT CHAIR OF THE FIRST EMPIRE,
DESIGNED BY LECONTE

being many and rich, they were fewer and less
ornate, sometimes made of carved wood instead of
metal, and painted a colour to imitate green bronze.

The coverings of the chairs and sofas of the period corresponded, and carpets, curtains, and also the decoration of walls and ceilings. Red, green and yellow silks embroidered or woven with wreaths, lyres, or the conventionalized honeysuckle in silver and gold were suitable for the richer kinds of seats.

The carved and gilt furniture was particularly splendid, and some of the massive throne-like chairs we still occasionally find, seem to remind us of a triumphant Maréchal of France during Napoleon's successful campaigns.

The Palace of Fontainebleau, about forty miles from Paris, is very rich in specimens of the best kind of Empire furniture, it was furnished by Napoleon in the days of his prosperity.

Since the First Empire there has been no pronounced style in French furniture. As fashion has changed it has been the mode to reproduce Henri Deux or Louis Quatorze, Louis Quinze or Louis Seize. Military expeditions and conquests have, from time to time, left their mark, as when the Tonking campaign caused the revival of a taste for Chinese models and shapes for furniture. Blackwood cabinets, tables and chairs were inlaid with mother-of-pearl and carved with fantastic designs; and later on there was an Algerian and Tunisian influence on some of the more fanciful articles of furniture, but the different epochs of taste which I have briefly referred to in this chapter are those which are the classic styles for French furniture and decoration.

Reproductions

The almost fabulous prices which within the last quarter of a century have been given for genuine examples of the best kinds of French furniture of the different styles reviewed in this chapter, have caused a great demand for copies and reproductions, and I now propose to add some notes about these. They may be roughly divided into three classes: 1. Those made to deceive the purchaser and to be passed off as genuine; 2. Those which are ordinary reproductions of furniture of the style; and, 3, Reproductions by the first *ébenistes* or cabinet makers and bronze artists of Paris, made not for the purpose of deception, but produced either in the execution of orders from wealthy amateurs, who want exact replicas of the finest specimens, which, being national property, cannot be purchased; or else as *tours de force* for the purpose of exhibition, or for sale to those who, unwilling or unable to pay several thousand pounds for a bureau or a commode of the epoch, are yet willing to give some two or three hundred pounds for a well-made piece of the best workmanship, correct in every detail as to design and faithfully reproduced from the original.

In the chapter on "faked" furniture I have said something about the first-named kind of reproduction, and in the last chapter of this book, containing some hints and cautions to the collector, I have added some remarks. With regard to the second class, they might again be subdivided into good, bad, and indifferent. If the reader wishes to have decorative furniture of the style he prefers, he must use his discretion in endeavouring to select that which is least pretentious, the nearest to the original, and that which is most free from the meretricious showy splendour which renders the cheaper kinds of imitations of good old French furniture so objectionable. It is quite possible to purchase for very moderate sums, good honest furniture with the graceful lines and curves of the Louis XV style, or the simpler modesty of the more severe Marie Antoinette period, but the selection should be made from those not too generously mounted or too lavishly inlaid.

It is about the third class that I feel I may be doing my reader some service in offering advice. Some of the reproductions of Boulle's work, of the cabinets and tables by Riesener, David Roentgen, Pasquier, Carlin, Leleu, Cressent, and others (a fairly complete list of whom has been given in my " History of Furniture"), are really works of art. If the reader has the means to buy, and the kind of house which will accommodate such beautiful specimens of the cabinet-maker's art, I would recommend them as an excellent investment of capital. They have been made by such masters as I have named earlier in this chapter, and neither pains nor expense have been spared to produce the best results. As time goes on and highly-skilled labour becomes more and more costly, such pieces as I am referring to will acquire a much greater value, especially as, if carefully preserved, they are allowed to acquire the improved tone that time gives to well gilt bronze and fine marqueterie.

Many of these rich pieces are only suitable for large mansions, since they have been copied from the originals intended for the salons of the kings, or their ministers and favourites, but some are of smaller and more modest proportions, and are excellent and most desirable acquisitions. They can only be found in the hands of the chief dealers, as they are necessarily costly, but they can be obtained at a fair price, and to my mind are much cheaper than the commoner copies produced in great quantities and sold for small sums.

CPSIA information can be obtained at www.ICGtesting.com
Printed in the USA
LVOW11s1158141114

413701LV00001B/14/P